Charles Dickens's

A Christmas Carol

Peter Leigh

Published in association with The Basic Skills Agency

Hodder & Stoughton

A MEMBER OF THE HODDER HEADLINE

Acknowledgements
Cover: Paul Cemmick
Illustrations: Jim Eldridge

Every effort has been made to trace copyright holders of material reproduced in this book. Any rights not acknowledged will be acknowledged in subsequent printings if notice is given to the publisher.

Orders; please contact Bookpoint Ltd, 39 Milton Park, Abingdon, Oxon OX14 4TD. Telephone: (44) 01235 400414, Fax: (44) 01235 400454. Lines are open from 9.00–6.00, Monday to Saturday, with a 24 hour message answering service. Email address: orders@bookpoint.co.uk

British Library Cataloguing in Publication Data
A catalogue record for this title is available from the British Library

ISBN 0 340 77459 2

First published 2000
Impression number 10 9 8 7 6 5 4 3 2 1
Year   2005 2004 2003 2002 2001 2000

Typeset by GreenGate Publishing Services, Tonbridge, Kent.
Printed in Great Britain for Hodder and Stoughton Educational, a division of Hodder Headline Plc, 338 Euston Road, London NW1 3BH, by Redwood Books, Trowbridge, Wilts

About the author

Charles Dickens was born in 1812,
and died in 1870.

He is still one of our most popular writers.
Films and television series are often
made from his stories.

About the people

Ebenezer Scrooge – a miser. He's very rich, but mean and
cruel to everyone.

Bob Cratchit –	Scrooge's clerk
Tiny Tim –	Bob's son
Marley's ghost –	The ghost of Scrooge's partner
Three Ghosts –	The Ghost of Christmas Past
	The Ghost of Christmas Present
	The Ghost of Christmas Future

Other people from Scrooge's past are in the story.

About the story

This is Dickens's best-loved story.
It's been filmed.
It's been on television,
and it's even been made into a musical.

It's Christmas Eve.
It's snowing and very cold.
Scrooge is working late.
He is counting money.
He is so mean
he is keeping Bob Cratchit working late.
Bob has a long scarf wrapped round him,
but he is still shivering.
Scrooge is so mean
he won't let Bob have a fire.

Finally it gets so late
that even Scrooge has to go home.
He turns to his clerk …

I   Marley's Ghost

'You'll want all day tomorrow, I suppose?'

'If that's all right, Sir.'

'It's not all right,
and it's not fair.
If I was to stop you half-a-crown for it,
you'd think yourself very ill-used, I'm sure?'

'Yes, Sir.'

half-a-crown – old money
ill-used – badly treated

'And yet you don't think me ill-used,
when I pay a day's wages for no work.'

'It's only once a year, Sir.'

'A poor excuse for picking a man's pocket
every twenty-fifth of December!
But I suppose you must have the whole day.
Be here even earlier next morning!'

Bob promised that he would.
Scrooge walked out with a growl.

Scrooge went home to bed.
He lived in rooms
which had once belonged
to Jacob Marley, his dead partner.
They were gloomy rooms,
in a gloomy building.
The building was old and dreary.
Nobody lived in it but Scrooge.
All the other rooms were offices.

On the door of this house was a knocker.
Now, there was nothing unusual
about this knocker
except that it was very large.

Also Scrooge had seen it night and morning
since he had lived there.
Also Scrooge had no imagination.
And yet when Scrooge
put his key in the lock of the door,
he saw not the knocker,
but Marley's face.

Marley's face!

dismal – grey and
dreary

With a dismal light about it.
Not angry or fierce,
but looking at Scrooge,
just as Marley used to look.

As Scrooge stared at it,
it was a knocker again.
He said 'Pooh, pooh!'
and closed the door with a bang.

The sound echoed through the house
like thunder.
Every room above,
every room below,
seemed to have an echo of its own.

Scrooge was not a man
to be frightened by echoes.
He locked the door,
and walked across the hall,
and up the stairs.

Up Scrooge went.
He didn't care
that it was very dark.
Darkness is cheap,
and Scrooge liked it.
But before he shut his heavy door,
he walked through his rooms
to see that all was right.

Sitting-room, bedroom, spare-room.
All as they should be.
Nobody under the table.
Nobody under the sofa.
A small fire in the grate.
Spoon and basin ready,

gruel – thin porridge

and a little saucepan of gruel upon the hob.
Nobody under the bed.
Nobody in the wardrobe.
Nobody in his dressing-gown.

cravat – an
old-fashioned tie

Quite satisfied he closed his door,
and locked himself in.
He took off his cravat,
and put on his dressing-gown and slippers,
and his night-cap.
He sat down before the very low fire
to take his gruel.

These bells were
used to call servants.
All old houses used
to have them.

As he leaned back in the chair,
he glanced at a bell
that hung in the room.
As he looked,
he saw this bell begin to swing.

Soon it rang out loudly,
and so did every bell in the house.
Then, deep down below,
there was a clanking noise.
It was as if some person
was dragging a heavy chain.

Then he heard the noise much louder,
on the floors below.
Then coming up the stairs.
Then coming straight towards his door.
It came on through the heavy door,
and a ghost passed into the room before his
eyes.

Marley's ghost!

This is what men
wore at the time.

transparent – see
through

The same face! The very same.
Marley in his pigtail,
usual waistcoat, tights, and boots.
His body was transparent.
Scrooge could look through his waistcoat,
and see the two buttons on his coat behind.

'How now,' said Scrooge very frightened.
'What do you want with me?'

'Much!'

It was Marley's voice,
no doubt about it.

'Who are you?'
'Ask me who I was.'
'Who were you then?'
'In life I was your partner, Jacob Marley.'
'Can you – can you sit down?'
'I can.'
'Do it then.'

The Ghost sat down
on the other side of the fireplace.

'Why do you trouble me?' said Scrooge
trembling.
'Why do ghosts walk the earth,
and why do they come to me?'

'The spirit of every man

walk abroad – go among

must walk abroad among his fellow-men,
and travel far and wide.
If that spirit does not do so in life,
it must do so after death.

He cannot tell Scrooge everything that he would like to.

I cannot tell you all I would.
A very little more is permitted to me.
I cannot rest,
I cannot stay,

linger – stay

I cannot linger anywhere.
My spirit never walked

counting-house – bank

beyond our counting-house.
In life my spirit never went
beyond our money-changing hole.
Weary journeys lie before me.'

'But you were always
a good man of business, Jacob,'
said Scrooge weakly.

'Business! Mankind was my business.
The common good was my business.
Charity, mercy, kindness,
were all my business.
My job was only a drop of water
in the ocean of my business!'

The Ghost held up its chain at arm's length,
and flung it heavily on the ground again.

Scrooge began to shake.

'You are chained,' he said.
'Tell me why?'

forge – to make
things out of metal,
like a blacksmith
does

'I wear the chain I forged in life,'
said the Ghost
'I made it link by link, yard by yard.
Do you know the weight and the length
of the chain you have made for yourself?
It was as heavy and as long as this
seven years ago.
You have worked hard on it since.'

Scrooge shook more and more.

'Hear me!' said the Ghost.
'My time is nearly gone.'

'I will.
But don't be hard upon me, Jacob! Please.'

'I am here tonight to warn you.
You still have one chance
of escaping my fate.'

'You were always a good friend to me.
Thank you!'

'You will be haunted by Three Spirits.'

'Is that the one chance you mentioned, Jacob?
I – I think I'd rather not.'

'Without them,
you cannot escape my fate!
Expect the first
when the bell strikes one.
You will see me no more.
But for your sake,
remember what has passed between us!'

The Ghost rose,
and walked backward from Scrooge.
At every step it took,
the window raised itself a little.
When the Ghost reached it,
it was wide open.
It floated out
through the self-opened window
into the bleak dark night.

The window opened
by itself.

Scrooge closed the window,
and examined the door
by which the Ghost had entered.
It was double locked.
He had locked it with his own hands.
Scrooge tried to say 'Pooh! Pooh!'
but stopped at 'Poo…'.
He went straight to bed,
and fell asleep on the instant.

on the instant –
straight away

II The First Spirit

When Scrooge woke
it was dark.

The church clock tolled
a deep, dark, hollow One!

Light flashed up in the room,
and the curtains of his bed were drawn back
by a strange figure.
It was like a child,
and yet at the same time,
like an old man.
Its hair was white,
and yet the face had not a wrinkle.

'Are you the Spirit, sir,
I was told to expect?'
'I am!'
'Who are you?'
'I am the Ghost of Christmas Past.'
'Long past?'
'No. Your past.
The things that you will see with me
are shadows of the things that have been.
Rise and walk with me.'

The Spirit touched his arm.
It was useless for Scrooge to argue,
or say that the hour was late,
or that the bed was warm,
or that it was freezing outside,
or that he only had his night-shirt on,
and that he had a cold as well.
The touch, though gentle,
was not to be resisted.

They passed through the wall,
and stood in the busy street of a city.
The decorations in the shops
showed it was Christmas time.

The Ghost stopped at a warehouse door.
He asked Scrooge, 'Do you know it?'

'Know it? I was apprenticed here!'

They went in.
An old gentleman in a large wig
was sitting behind a desk.

'Why, it's old Fezziwig!' cried Scrooge.
'Bless his heart!
It's Fezziwig alive again!'

The old gentleman laid down his pen,
and glanced at the clock.
He rubbed his hands,
and gave a great laugh.

'Ho, there!' he called.
'Ebenezer! Dick!'

A young man came in –
it was the living, moving picture
of Scrooge, as he used to be.
The other apprentice came after.

'Dick Wilkins, to be sure,'
said Scrooge to the Ghost.
'My old fellow apprentice!
Bless me, yes. There he is.
He was very fond of me, was Dick.
Poor Dick! Dear, dear!'

'Ho, my boys,' said Fezziwig.
'No more work tonight!
It's Christmas Eve!

Clear away, my lads,
and let's have lots of room here.'

Clear away?
It was done in a minute.
Everything was packed away,
the floor swept and watered,
the lamps lit,
and the fire piled high.
The warehouse was
snug and warm and dry and bright.

The floor was swept
and mopped.

In came the fiddler,
and tuned up, like fifty stomach-aches.
In came Mrs Fezziwig, one vast smile.
In came the three Miss Fezziwigs,
beaming and loveable.
In came the six young men
whose hearts they broke.
In came all the young men and women
who worked for Fezziwig.
In came the maid,
with her cousin, the baker.
In came the cook,
with her brother's best friend, the milkman.
In they all came, one after another.
Some shyly, some boldly,
some gracefully, some awkwardly,
some pushing, some pulling.
In they all came,
anyhow and every how.

In the days before
stereos or discos,
the music for parties
was live – in this
case a 'fiddler' or
violinist.

And away they went,
twenty couples at once,
hands half round
and back again the other way,
down the middle and up again,
round and round and round.

There were dances,
and there were forfeits,
and more dances,
and there was cake,
and there was hot punch,
and there was a great piece of roast beef,
and there was a great piece of boiled ham,
and there were mince pies,
and plenty of beer.

Scrooge enjoyed it all.
He remembered everything just as it was.
His heart and soul were there,
in the dancing, in the games,
and with his friends.
It was not until the party was ending
and Mr and Mrs Fezziwig were saying
goodbye to everyone,
that he remembered the Ghost.

'It's very easy,' said the Ghost,
'to make these silly people happy.'

'*Easy*?' said Scrooge.

'Why should everybody like Fezziwig?
He hasn't spent very much money on them.'

'It wasn't that,' said Scrooge.
'It wasn't the money.
He could make us happy.
He had the power to make everyone happy.
Money wasn't important.
Money ...'

He stopped.

'What's the matter?' said the Ghost.
'Nothing.'
'Something, I think?'
'No. No. I should like to be able
to say a word to my clerk just now!
That's all.'
'My time grows short,' said the Ghost.
'Quick!'

The scene changed once more.
Again Scrooge saw himself.
He was older now –
a man in the prime of life.
He was not alone.
Sitting by his side
was a fair young girl in a black dress.
There were tears in her eyes.

idol – something to
be worshipped

'It matters very little to you,' she said.
'Another idol has replaced me
in your eyes.'

'What other idol?'

'A golden one.
You have changed towards me.
When we became engaged
you were another man.'

'I was a boy.'

'You have changed.
I have not.
If you were free today,
you would not marry me,
a girl without money.
I release you from our engagement.
With a full heart,
for the love of him
you once were.
May you be happy
in the life you have chosen.'

She left him.
And they parted.

'Spirit', cried Scrooge.
'Show me no more.
Remove me from this place.'

'I told you these were shadows
of the things that have been,' said the Ghost.
'They are what they are.
Do not blame me.'

'Remove me!
I cannot bear it!
Leave me!
Take me back!'

He was suddenly very tired,
and was in his own bedroom again.
He had barely time to fall into bed,
before he sank into a heavy sleep.

III The Second Spirit

Scrooge awoke in his own bedroom.
But what a change!

The walls and ceiling were hung
with holly and ivy and mistletoe.
A mighty blaze went roaring up the chimney.
The floor was piled high
with turkeys, geese, sausages,
mince pies and Christmas puddings.
On top of it all sat a Giant.

'I am the Ghost of Christmas Present,' he cried.
'Look upon me.
You have never seen
the like of me before.'

'Never,' said Scrooge.

'Touch my robe!'

Scrooge did as he was told,
and held it fast.
The room vanished,
and they stood in the city streets
on a snowy Christmas morning.

People were clearing the snow,
laughing and chatting.
Children were throwing snowballs,
and in the distance, church bells were ringing.

Scrooge and the Ghost passed by invisible.
They went straight to Bob Cratchit's,
Scrooge's clerk.
Mrs Cratchit was laying the table,
helped by her daughter.
Young Peter Cratchit was sticking a fork
into a saucepan of potatoes.

Two smaller Cratchits came tearing in –
they had smelt the goose.

'Wherever is your precious father, then?'
said Mrs Cratchit.
'And your brother, Tiny Tim?'
'Here's father!'
cried the two younger Cratchits.

In came Bob
with his scarf hanging down in front,
and his threadbare clothes all brushed,
and Tiny Tim upon his shoulder.
Poor Tiny Tim!
He had a little crutch,
and his legs were supported
by an iron frame.

Bob set him down.
The two younger Cratchits
hustled him off to the kitchen
to hear the pudding singing.

Christmas puddings have to be steamed for a long time. It can sound like singing.

'And how did little Tim behave?'
said Mrs Cratchit, after they had gone.

'As good as gold,' said Bob, 'and better.
He gets thoughtful
sitting by himself so much.
He thinks the strangest things
you ever heard.
He told me, coming home,
that he hoped the people
saw him in the church,
because he was a cripple.
Then they might remember
on Christmas Day,
who made the lame walk
and the blind see.'

Bob's voice shook
when he said this.
It shook a little more
when he said that Tiny Tim
was growing stronger.

The little crutch was heard upon the floor,
and back came Tiny Tim
to his stool beside the fire.

The gravy was made,
the potatoes mashed,
the apple-sauce sweetened.

Bob took Tiny Tim
beside him at the table,
and the goose was brought in.

The goose was the best and Bob liked the way his wife had cooked it.

There never was such a goose!
Bob said he didn't believe
there ever was such a goose cooked.
All said how tender it was,
and how good it tasted,
and how big it was,
and how cheap.
There was enough for the whole family.

They cleared the table and Mrs Cratchit went to get pudding.

And now the plates were changed.
Mrs Cratchit went out to get the pudding
by herself.
She couldn't bear anyone with her.
Suppose it should not be done enough!
Suppose it should break in getting it out!
Suppose someone had stolen it
while they were at the goose!

There was a great deal of steam,
and Mrs Cratchit came back,
flushed, but smiling proudly.

She carried the pudding,
flaming with brandy,
and topped with Christmas holly.

'Oh, a wonderful pudding!' said
Bob Cratchit.
'The best pudding ever!
Mrs Cratchit said there might be
too much flour.
Everybody had something to say about it –
its flavour or its richness.
Nobody said that it was a very small
pudding for such a large family.

Dinner was finished.

At last the dinner was done,
and the table cleared.
Bob raised his glass.
'A Merry Christmas to us all!'
'To us all!' said the family.
'God bless us every one!'
said Tiny Tim the last of all.

Bob raised his glass again.
'I give you Mr Scrooge,
the Founder of the Feast.'

the Founder – the
one who made it
possible

Scrooge raised his head
on hearing his own name.

But Mrs Cratchit cried,
'The Founder of the Feast indeed!
I wish I had him here.
I'd give him a piece of my mind
to feast upon!'

'My dear,' said Bob,
'The children! Christmas Day!'

'It should be Christmas Day
to drink the health
of such a stingy, hard, unfeeling man.
You know he is, Bob.
Nobody knows it better than you.'

'My dear! Christmas Day.'

'I'll drink his health
for your sake, and not for his.
He'll be very merry
and very happy, I have no doubt!'

And the children drank the toast after her.

Then there were stories,
and laughter, and songs.
And so it went on.

There was nothing high class in this.
They were an ordinary family.
They were not well dressed.
There were holes in their shoes.
Their clothes were secondhand.
But they were happy, grateful,
and pleased to be with one another.

As they began to fade from view,
Scrooge had his eye on them,
and especially on Tiny Tim,
till the last.

He was left alone
in an open place.
The Spirit had vanished.
Scrooge looked around.
Coming towards him
was a solemn figure,
draped and hooded.
It came like a mist along the ground.

IV The Third Spirit

The figure was in deep black
from head to toe.
Scrooge could see no face or figure
except one outstretched hand.
The Spirit neither spoke nor moved.

'You are the Ghost of Christmas Future,'
said Scrooge.
'Of all the Spirits I fear you most.
Will you not speak to me?'

It gave him no reply.
The hand was pointed straight before them.

'Lead on,' said Scrooge. 'Lead on.'

They didn't seem to enter the city,
the city seemed to spring up around them.

Bob Cratchit's house.
Quiet. Very quiet.
The two little Cratchits were as still as statues.
Peter had a book in front of him.
The mother and daughter were sewing.
Surely they were very quiet!

Peter read out loud,
"And He took a child,
and set him in the midst of them."

The mother laid her work upon the table.
She put her hand up to her face.

'The colour hurts my eyes,' she said.

She pretends it's
sewing that has
made her eyes red
and sore, and not
crying.

It was not the colour.
It was poor Tiny Tim!

'They're better now.
The candle makes them weak.
I wouldn't show my weak eyes
to your father for all the world,
when he comes home.
It must be near his time.'

'Past it rather,' said Peter
shutting up the book.
'But I think he walks a little slower now
than he used to.'

'I have known him walk with –
– with Tiny Tim on his shoulder,
very fast indeed!'
'And so have I,' cried Peter. 'Often.'
'And so have I,' said another.
So had all.

'But he was very light to carry,
and his father loved him so,
so that it was no trouble …
no trouble.
There is your father now.'

Bob came in, still in his long scarf.
He sat down.
The two smaller Cratchits got up on his knees,
and each laid a little cheek against his face,
as if to say,
'Don't mind it, father. Don't be upset.'

Bob spoke very cheerfully.
He looked at the sewing,
and said how well it was done,
and how quickly.
They would be done long before Sunday,
he said.

'Sunday? You went today, then, Bob?'

Yes, my dear,' said Bob.
'I wish you could have gone.
It would have done you good
to see how green a place it is.
But you'll see it often.
I promised him
that I would walk there on a Sunday.
My little, little child! My little child!'

He broke down all at once.
He couldn't help it.

The scene began to fade.

'Spirit,' said Scrooge. 'Tell me!
Are these the shadows
of things that *will* be?
Or are they the shadows
of things that *may* be, only?'

The Ghost said nothing.

They were in a dismal, ruined churchyard.
The Ghost stood among the graves,
and pointed down to one.

'I am not the man I was,' cried Scrooge.
'Tell me that if I change my life,
I can change these things
that you have shown me.'

The Ghost did not move.
Scrooge crept towards it,
trembling as he went.
He followed the finger
to a neglected grave.
On the stone was written
'EBENEZER SCROOGE'.

23

'I will honour Christmas.
I will try to keep it all year.
I have learnt the lesson.
Only tell me,' Scrooge begged,
'that I can wash away
the writing on this stone.'

As Scrooge reached out towards the Ghost,
it changed.
It shrunk, collapsed,
and dwindled into a bedpost.

dwindle – reduce to
nothing

Yes! And the bedpost was his own.
The bed was his own.
The room was his own.
Best, and happiest of all,
the time before him was his own,
time to make up for everything.

He ran to the window,
opened it, and put out his head.
No fog, no mist, no night!
Clear, bright, golden day!

'What's today?' called Scrooge
to a boy below.
'Eh?'
'What's today, my fine fellow?'
'Today? Why, CHRISTMAS DAY.'

'It's Christmas Day!
I haven't missed it.
Hallo, my fine fellow!'

'Hallo!'
'Do you know the shop
in the next street? On the corner?'
'Yes!'

'What an intelligent boy!
A remarkable boy!
Do you know
whether they've sold the prize turkey,
that was hanging up there?'
'What, the one as big as me?'
'What a delightful boy!
It's a pleasure to talk to him.
Yes!'
'It's hanging there now.'
'Is it? Go and buy it.'
'Get lost!' said the boy.
'No, no, I am serious.
Go and buy it.
Come back with the man,
and I'll give you a shilling.
Come back with him
in less than five minutes,
and I'll give you half-a-crown.'

The boy was off like a shot.

'I'll send it to Bob Cratchit's.
He shan't know who sent it.
It's the size of Tiny Tim.
It'll be such a joke!'

He got dressed all in his best.
When the man arrived
he sent him on to Bob Cratchit's.
Then he went out into the streets.

The people were about, by now.
Scrooge gave everyone a delighted smile.
He looked so happy
that three or four people said,
'Good morning, Sir!
A merry Christmas to you!'
Scrooge often said afterwards,
that of all the happy sounds he had heard,
those were the happiest.

He went to church,
and walked about the streets.
He talked to the people
hurrying to and fro.

He patted children on the head.
He looked down into the kitchens of the
houses, and up to the windows.
Everything gave him pleasure.
He never dreamed that any walk –
that anything –
could give him so much happiness.

The next day he was at the office early.
He had to be there,
and catch Bob Cratchit coming late!
That's what he had set his heart on.

And he did it!
The clock struck nine.
No Bob.
A quarter past. Still no Bob.
Bob was a full eighteen minutes late.

His hat was off
before he opened the door.
And his scarf.

in a jiffy – in a
second

He was on his stool in a jiffy,
and driving away with his pen,
as if he was trying to overtake nine o'clock.

'Hello,' growled Scrooge. 'What do you mean
by coming here at this time of day?'

'I am very sorry, Sir.
I am late.'

'You are! Step this way, if you please.'

'It's only once a year, Sir.
It shall not be repeated.'

'Now, I'll tell you what, my friend.
I am not going to stand for
this sort of thing any more.
And therefore –'
here Scrooge gave Bob
a great dig in the ribs –
'– and therefore I am going to
raise your salary!'

Bob was speechless.

'A merry Christmas, Bob,' said Scrooge,
and clapped him on the back.
'A merrier Christmas
than I have given you,
for many a year.
I'll raise your salary,
and help your struggling family.
We'll discuss it this afternoon
over a Christmas drink.
Make up the fires, Bob Cratchit,
and buy a second coal-scuttle.'

coal-scuttle – for
storing coal

Scrooge was better than his word.
He did it all,
and much more.
To Tiny Tim,
who did NOT die,
he was a second father.
He was as good a friend,
as good a master,
and as good a man as any.
Some laughed to see the change in him,
but his own heart laughed too,
and that was quite enough for him.

And he never again,
saw another SPIRIT!